Original title:
Purpose Found in the Most Unlikely Places

Copyright © 2025 Creative Arts Management OÜ
All rights reserved.

Author: Tobias Sterling
ISBN HARDBACK: 978-1-80566-238-9
ISBN PAPERBACK: 978-1-80566-533-5

Rainbows from Ruins

In a junkyard, I found a shoe,
Its missing mate was on a barbecue.
Who knew that trash could be a delight?
Sparkling colors in the dull moonlight.

Old tires stacked like pancakes high,
Turned into swings, I soared to the sky!
Found a bicycle with no working gear,
But joy brought laughter, no sign of fear.

Echoes of Forgotten Corners

A dusty corner hid an old hat,
Now it's a throne for the neighborhood cat.
Forgotten treasures beneath the grime,
Here I found my muse, lost in time.

A teapot chipped but full of cheer,
Served tea to friends who gathered near.
Each sip a giggle, each laugh a tease,
In forgotten corners, joy's sure to please.

Gold in the Gutter

Saw a glimmer where the pigeons play,
In the city's gutter, what a display!
A bottle cap, shiny and round,
A treasure that made my day profound.

Clumsy pigeons, they strutted with flair,
As I dubbed them models in mid-air.
Each sparkle told a story anew,
Beauty hidden, just waiting for you.

Blossoms Amidst the Weeds

In a patch of weeds, blooms stood tall,
Who knew they'd be the life of the ball?
Moments of glory in a world so gray,
These wildflowers danced in a joyful ballet.

Scarred pavement became a canvas bright,
Graffiti art sprouting in the night.
Laughter echoed in the strife,
Found in places, bursting with life.

Discoveries in an Ordinary Cup

In a mug that's got a chip,
I found a world to make me flip.
There's coffee swirling tales of glee,
And a stray hair from Auntie Lee.

Sipping all the weird coconut,
I wondered if it's time to strut.
With every sip, a laugh is brewed,
Who knew my cup was so well-mooded?

Glimmers of Joy in Marching Bands

With a tuba blaring loud and proud,
The band marched on, a rowdy crowd.
A trumpet honked just like a duck,
And everyone erupted in good luck.

Their feet stumbled, a misstep here,
Turns into dance, oh, what a cheer!
Drumsticks flew like overcooked fries,
We laughed till we nearly cried.

Lessons in the Library of Shadows

Among the books, I found my muse,
A ghost that cheekily refuses to snooze.
It whispered secrets, wild and deep,
Suggested snacks, and then a sweep.

Each dusty tome hid giggles galore,
With tales of wizards who used the floor.
In silenced corners, laughter echoed,
Turns out the shadows love a good show.

Unseen Colors in a Gray World

In a world draped in shades of gray,
A rainbow skateboard rolled my way.
It whispered jokes, it spun around,
Made the mundane a circus bound.

A field of grass, oh, what a sight,
Sprouted daisies with furry might.
Each petal giggled at the fog,
Turns out life's a cheerful smog!

Whispers from Forgotten Roads

In a shoe that once held a foot,
A lost sock squeaks 'Not yet, shoo!'
A tumbleweed rolls by laughing loud,
Saying 'Keep walking, don't feel too proud.'

Old tires gossip in ditches deep,
Telling tales of the dreams they keep.
A raccoon strums on a hubcap bright,
Finding rhythm in the moon's soft light.

Vendors sell hopes with a wink and jest,
Adding joy to the old road's quest.
An unlit lamp with a flicker of cheer,
Whispers of adventures waiting near.

With each turn, a chuckle or two,
Life's a circus; we're the crew.
So stroll along those winding ways,
And hear what the forgotten road says.

Beneath the Cracked Sidewalk

In the cracks where the daisies peek,
A curious worm begins to speak.
'Life's a party beneath your feet,
With dance-offs and snacks, oh what a treat!'

A lost penny rolls with a smirk,
'Finders keepers!' it seems to quirk.
'I'm the luckiest charm in this place,
Just try to steal my shiny grace!'

A lollipop stick plans a parade,
With ants as marchers, all unafraid.
They line up with confetti of dust,
Creating a scene that's simply a must!

So step lightly and don't miss the fun,
Even cracks can be races to run.
There's laughter and joy on this quirky street,
Where the mundane turns into a treat.

Treasures in the Attic Dust

Up in the attic where shadows grow,
An old guitar twangs, 'Let's start a show!'
A pirate hat waves 'Avast, me mates!'
While forgotten dolls hold high-stakes debates.

A trunk full of shoes with stories to tell,
Each pair has danced, oh, so very well.
A teddy bear claims he's a knight so bold,
Guarding treasures of stories double gold.

Cobbwebbed wonders hum tunes of cheer,
While old books whisper 'Read us, dear!'
Forgotten relics sing with delight,
In dust and shadows, they hold their light.

So rummage through layers where memories cling,
As laughter erupts, let your spirit sing.
In every corner, there's fun to be found,
Within the chaos, joy knows no bounds.

When the Storm Unveils the Rainbow

When thunder rolls like a drummer late,
And puddles form a wobbly skate,
A worm in boots slides down the lane,
Giggling softly, 'I love the rain!'

Clouds throw shade as they wear their frown,
But a sunbeam sneaks in, wearing a crown.
Daisies sway to the raindrop beat,
While snails glide by on a dance-off street.

A rainbow arches in the sky so wide,
Like a bridge for dreams to take a ride.
'Join us!' shouts a kite on the run,
As laughter erupts in the warm, wet fun.

So let storms come with their mighty roar,
For after the rain, there's always more.
Find joy in colors that splash and play,
Funny surprises brighten the gray.

Routes Less Traveled by Wayfarers

I wandered down a path less bright,
Where squirrels danced and took to flight.
A sign that read, "This road's a mess!"
But a pizza truck? Now that's success!

My friends all napped on sunny grass,
While I chased geese, they stood in class.
A compass lost, but that's okay,
I found a dog who wanted to play!

The road was bumpy, the signs were wrong,
Yet laughter echoed, a silly song.
An ant parade, marching in style,
All made my wandering quite worthwhile!

So here's to paths that twist and wind,
Where joy awaits in every find.
Next time you roam, just let it be,
The best detours might set you free!

Nature's Secrets in the Cracks of Pavement

Between the bricks, a flower bloomed,
A sprightly chap who never gloomed.
He cracked that ground with all his might,
And said, "Why not? The sun feels right!"

A worm in specs looked up and cheered,
"You're bright, my friend, have never feared!"
But then he slipped, and oh, the shame,
As raindrops sent him down the drain!

The mice held court in alleyway,
With tales of cheese that got away.
In every crevice, life abounds,
An urban jungle, laughter sounds!

So if you stumble on this scene,
Where cracks and critters lurk between,
Just stop, look close, and you may find,
The joy in places, everyone's blind!

Whispers in the Attic

In the attic, dust gathers thick,
A box of toys, oh that's the trick!
With action figures, robots too,
They plot a coup, who knew they'd brew?

A teddy bear with tales to tell,
Of secret lands, where he did dwell.
He whispered low, "I seek a friend,
To join me, on adventures without end!"

The old vinyls spun their tunes,
While moths danced together like loons.
A hidden map, a treasure chest,
All found in places you'd never guess!

Though stuff may rust, and tapes may hiss,
There's more to life than just a miss.
In every corner, find delight,
In dusty planes, dreams take flight!

The Light Beneath the Stone

Beneath a rock, a glow does shine,
A party's happening, oh how divine!
The frogs are dancing, the crickets sing,
A riot of colors - what a swing!

A party hat on a sly little mouse,
With snacks galore in this tiny house.
"Join us now, don't just peep!"
He winked at me, said, "Don't you sleep!"

A ladybug served drinks with flair,
While ants lined up for the dandy fair.
To think a stone could guard such fun,
In hidden nooks, bright days are spun!

So next time you walk, don't overlook,
These playful scenes tucked in every nook.
For light can spark in shadowed places,
With laughter ringing, joy embraces!

The Warmth of Worn Hands

In a café where old folks sit,
A grumpy man without a wit.
He shares a grin, gives a nod,
His doughnut stash—there's the odd!

Beneath a hat, his hair's a mess,
He always smells of sweet finesse.
Yet, share a tale, and life's a dance,
With old hands, he gives dreams a chance.

The Magic of Mundanity

At the grocery store, what a sight,
A toddler's tantrum, a cat in flight!
Amidst the aisles, a dance unfolds,
Boring shopping? Not when laughter's sold!

A lady's list, so fancy and neat,
But she forgets which aisle for meat.
In the humdrum, joy can ignite,
A cart race? Now that's pure delight!

Kindness in a Cracked Cup

At a café with chipped porcelain,
A barista spills coffee—pure mayhem!
But a smile spreads, no one's disgraced,
In this chaos, a kindness embraced.

The cup may crack, but spirits soar,
As laughter brews on the café floor.
"Who wants tea?"—everyone's in line,
In quirky cups, connections shine!

The Charm of the Abandoned

An old house with windows grim,
Whispers tales when the lights dim.
A cat sneezes in a dusty chair,
Life's charm nestled in the wear and tear.

In forgotten spots, a treasure seen,
A rusty swing—what joy can glean!
For in the wreckage, stories bloom,
Finding laughter in the gloom!

Solace in the Scraps

In a pile of leftovers, I found my muse,
A half-eaten taco? My creative ruse!
With pickled onions and guacamole too,
In the fridge's deep depths, inspiration grew.

Old socks and a sock puppet made me laugh,
They held meetings for a strange, silly staff.
A collection of crumbs becomes my parade,
Whispering secrets, "Don't let dreams fade."

The Unfurling of the Unnoticed

Underneath the couch, a remote takes a seat,
It holds the key to laughter and to heat.
A sandwich from last week? A crusty treasure,
Unfolding stories—of loss and of pleasure.

Found a rubber band ball, oh what a sight,
It bounced on the floor, snug and tight.
It gathered dust like wisdom in time,
Rolling through chaos, it danced in rhyme.

Clarity in the Clutter

Surrounded by laundry, a sock stands tall,
It waved like a flag—come one, come all!
Among paper piles, a path I carve,
Where lost items dwell, I always starve.

A spoon that snuck off for a romantic cheese,
In the fridge it giggles with deli and peas.
Amidst the chaos, hilarity breeds,
Finding joy in the mess, it's all that one needs.

Songs of the Subtle

Quiet outside, but loud in my head,
A dusty old book told me to tread.
Its spine cracked with laughter, pages turned bright,
Whispering tales of the day and the night.

The cat in her box sings soft lullabies,
As buttons and straws dance under the skies.
Hiding in plain sight, inspiration brings,
Wonders unfolding, as laughter takes wings.

The Forgotten Art of Gathering Twigs

In the woods, where squirrels dance,
I gather twigs while wearing pants.
My pockets bulge, a sight so grand,
Who knew this art would be in demand?

A stick for poking, a stick for prods,
Crafting a throne fit for woodland gods.
The neighbors stare as they walk their dogs,
My twig collection beats their boring logs!

In twirls and knots, nature's gifts,
I conduct symphonies, the wind uplifts.
A patchwork crown atop my head,
All hail the twig king, this throne, well spread!

So next you stroll through the leafy maze,
Think of the twigs and their quirky ways.
If I can find joy in such small things,
Imagine the laughter that this day brings!

Voices Carried by the Wind

A tumbleweed rolls, with tales to tell,
Caught in the breeze, it dances so well.
It hums a tune from a far-off place,
A croon of chaos in nature's race.

With every whistle, a chuckle erupts,
As if the trees have been eavesdropping up.
The leaves laugh back, a rustling cheer,
Stories grow taller when winds draw near.

I heard a squirrel squawking about,
A gossiping critter, oh what a scout!
The whispers blend, a cacophony bright,
Voices of nature, a comical sight.

So let's raise a glass to the wind's delight,
Who carries our chuckles, both day and night.
Next time you're lost, just pause, and you'll find,
The giggles of nature can brighten your mind!

Reflections in a Puddle's Eye

Oh look at me in that puddle wide,
I see my face, and I can't hide.
A splash of mud, my new hairdo,
Who knew reflections could be so askew?

A duck swims by, quacking with glee,
Is that a fashion statement, or just me?
We waddle and dance under cloudy grey,
Making spillovers in a goofy display.

The sky frowns down, I stick out my tongue,
My silly face is forever young.
Mirror, mirror, so splashy and bright,
Tell me the truths of this splashy sight!

So if ever you find a puddle near,
Jump right in, and let out a cheer!
For in every ripple, there's laughter to see,
Reflections of joy, just wild and free!

The Soft Glow of a Candle in the Dark

In the corner sits a flickering flame,
Casting shadows, playing their game.
A tiny dance with the safety cap,
Textures of night in a cozy lap.

I raise my toast to this buttery glow,
As it whispers secrets, both fast and slow.
Yet here in the dark, I find a thrill,
Who knew a candle could bring such chill?

It tipsy-twirls, like it's had some wine,
Wobbly and joyful, oh that's just fine.
The aroma of wax fills up the nook,
Maybe it's time for a spooky book!

So let's all gather for a night out bright,
With giggles and stories that banish fright.
For in shadows or light, we share our spark,
Even tiny flames can light up the dark!

Victory in the Void

In the dark where socks do hide,
A lone left shoe takes a ride.
It dreams of paired ballet at night,
Yet dances solo with pure delight.

A spoon in the drawer feels quite grand,
Dancing with forks, it makes a band.
They serenade the lonely plate,
As jellybeans join to celebrate.

In the empty fridge, a lone yogurt sighs,
Dreaming of snacks and midnight fries.
It finds a friend in a sad old cake,
Together they plot a daring escape.

The lost keys jingle a merry tune,
Inviting mugs beneath the moon.
In the chaos of things that don't align,
They all find joy in a life divine.

Smiles from the Shadows

Beneath the couch, where dust bunnies play,
A remote control dreams of a game day.
It chuckles softly, 'oh what a tease,'
As it schemes to escape with the car keys.

A half-eaten slice of pizza waits,
For a hungry mouse with lofty fates.
They laugh about the toppings' plight,
As they share tales of the Friday night.

The old lamp in the corner gleams bright,
With a gossiping bulb, it spreads delight.
Whispers echo of missed romance,
Giving shadows a chance to dance.

In the closet, forgotten shoes plot,
They yearn for a stroll on the boulevard shot.
With laces tied in a jovial spree,
They clamber out to feel the free.

Tales of Timid Trains

In the station, a timid train stands still,
Dreaming of tracks at the top of a hill.
It's scared of the tunnels and darkened curves,
Yet yearns for the journeys it surely deserves.

A whistle blows, it quakes with fright,
Yet chugs away into the twilight.
The passengers giggle, the humor's rich,
As they ride with a train on a daring pitch.

Through the woods, it slips and slides,
Encounters a frog, who hops and glides.
Together they laugh at the world so wide,
In their whimsical dance, they find their stride.

Timid no longer, the train pulls ahead,
All thanks to a leap and a frog's little thread.
With joy in its engine, it reaches a peak,
In each quirky moment, happiness speaks.

Revelations Amidst the Ruins

In a garden where weeds spin stories anew,
A broken pot wears a flower crown too.
It chuckles at being tossed away,
Now it reigns where the sunbeams play.

A rusty bike frame, no longer complete,
Hopes for a joyride down the sweet street.
It dreams of racing with vibrant glee,
As squirrels cheer on from the old oak tree.

Amidst the rubble, a lonely old shoe,
Finds a partner in a glove, worn and blue.
Their tales of mischief fill the air,
As they giggle at every passerby stare.

In the ashes where laughter used to reign,
New friendships bloom, breaking the chain.
In the quirkiest ruins, they learn to thrive,
Amidst every treble, they find the drive.

Melodies of the Misplaced

In a sock drawer, music plays,
An old tune hums through funky ways.
Laundry left, a bluesy croon,
That rhythm's got me dancing soon.

Rubbing elbows, forks and spoons,
They jam together, crafting tunes.
A spatula sings in perfect pitch,
Who knew the kitchen felt so rich?

Beneath the couch, a lost guitar,
Strumming softly, raising the bar.
Even crumbs join, they shake and sway,
The dust bunnies host a show today!

In chaos, joy begins to bloom,
A concert held in every room.
So when you can't find your dear stuff,
Just listen close, it's never rough.

Candlelight in the Clutter

Amidst the chaos of my desk,
A flicker shines, a light grotesque.
Papers piled high, but here it glows,
A candle's dance, a wild show.

An old mop sits beside a pen,
Its handle wags, it feels like Zen.
With wax and wax, it spins and sways,
In this mess, forget the gray days!

Tangled cords, a symphony start,
It's easy to lose the humble heart.
But there's magic in the spilled ink,
Just take a breath, and let it sink.

So let the clutter rise up tall,
Find delight where shadows fall.
For every mess can shine anew,
In the candlelight, find your view.

Elegance in Erosion

A cracked pot with flowers blooming,
In its flaws, nature's grooming.
Potholes dance with wild delight,
Creating art in the dark of night.

Rusty bikes sit weathered aside,
Yet childhood memories still take pride.
With wheels askew and frames so bent,
They roll through laughter, minds content.

A frayed rug underfoot does sway,
Worn threads tell stories of lively play.
Every scratch, a wink, a grin,
In life's messiness, a big win.

So in the cracks where time has shown,
There's beauty found, magic grown.
Embrace the flaws, the dirt, the cheer,
In erosion's hand, we draw near.

A Glimpse Through the Grime

Behind the glass, a world awry,
Mice in top hats, oh my my!
There's a party held in the muck,
Even roaches get a bit of luck.

Amidst the dust bunnies' wild tarot,
Pigeons converse about tomorrow.
Each smudge paints dreams in vivid hue,
Finding joy in the things we rue.

A forgotten chair wears a tiara,
With cushions dancing like a ballerina.
They leap and twirl, despite the plight,
In the cluttered corners, pure delight.

So take a peek at what you see,
In the grime, there's glee for free.
Through the mess, find whimsy's play,
In laughter's echo, lose your way.

Petals on a Windy Path

A squirrel dressed as a lawyer struts,
Arguing with the chips in the nuts.
Sunlight giggles as shadows flee,
Even a tree knows when to be free.

A kite stuck high in a branchy grasp,
Whistles a tune, the wind's fun gasp.
Dancing flowers join in the spree,
Nature's stage, wild and carefree.

Beauty in Brokenness

A vase cracked, holds secrets inside,
Where mismatched blooms choose to abide.
A dog in a tutu, looking perplexed,
Stumbles and fumbles, always unvexed.

The clock chimed eleven, then jumped to three,
Time's just a jester, who cares? Let it be!
Laughter bubbles, like soda and fizz,
In the oddest spots, we find our bliss!

Fortune in the Fray

A cat with a crown, ruling the night,
Claims the best spot, it's quite a sight.
A mix-up of socks, a sock puppet stew,
Turns laundry into a circus, who knew?

Mice in tuxedos throw a grand ball,
While the dog takes a nap, they're having a ball!
In this chaotic dance of delight,
We find treasure in laughter, all wrong feels right.

The Unraveled Thread

A sweater unwound, now a cat's delight,
Chasing the yarn with all of its might.
A pancake flipped high, it lands on a car,
Impromptu breakfast, now that's bizarre!

Buttons are rebels, they roll down the street,
Joining a parade that can't be beat.
In the mess and the chaos, we uncover the glee,
Life's greatest riches are often just free.

The Secret Lives of Broken Things

A toaster's dreams of flight at dawn,
It longs to soar, yet it's just a pawn.
With every crumb, a tiny cheer,
Who knew a toast could shed a tear?

A shoe missing its mate, quite bizarre,
Dancing solo, a little star.
With scuffs and scars, it takes a leap,
In puddles of joy, the secrets keep.

A clock that chimes without a time,
Ticking away, in its own rhyme.
It dreams of races, yet sits so still,
Counting the moments, against its will.

From broken glass to lopsided art,
They all have stories, play their part.
In the garage, in the attic's breath,
Life, and laughter, from what seems left.

Laughter in the Empty Hallways

Echoes bounce off silent walls,
Where laughter lingers and softly calls.
An old shoe slides with a jazzy twist,
In hallways where sunlight likes to mist.

A forgotten chair with a wobbly leg,
Sways to a tune, a jellyfish beg.
The dust has dances, the cobwebs giggle,
In the corners where shadows wiggle.

Mops and brooms form a funky crew,
They sweep out laughter like it's brand new.
In the corners, they tell silly jokes,
While the fridge hums with tales of yolks.

Each step's a chuckle, every path a grin,
In empty spaces, the fun begins.
With whispers of joy in each dark spot,
Making the mundane completely forgot.

Finding Stars Under the City Lights

Amidst the chaos, a cat takes its stroll,
Wearing a crown made of a tinfoil bowl.
It pounces on shadows, with regal grace,
As streets twinkle like a cosmic embrace.

The bus stop bench, a throne of glee,
Where friends share secrets and oddity.
A sandwich steals a heart with a smile,
In the city's hum, they linger a while.

Streetlights flicker like fireflies bright,
Guiding lost souls with their gentle light.
A gum wrapper dances, a paper kite,
In the city's buzz, everything's right.

Beneath the lamps, the laughter collides,
Starlit dreams where the fun resides.
In the mundane, magic's lightly tucked,
Under city lights, hilarity's plucked.

The Serenity of a Tattered Book

In pages worn, a tale unfolds,
A hero's blunders, brave and bold.
With coffee stains and tales quite sweet,
Each chapter hums to a silly beat.

A bookmark lost, like time gone loose,
While characters trip without excuse.
Every plot twist brings a chuckle out,
Questions of life, with a wink and shout.

Dusty shelves share secrets unspun,
With every read, the silliness won.
A library's echo of laughter's grace,
In every book, a familiar face.

Tattered tales bring a calming peace,
Where the absurd and wise find their release.
In ink and paper, joy intertwines,
Life's silly riddles played through lines.

The Wisdom of Worn Boots

Old boots by the door, a tale to tell,
Of puddles jumped and folks who fell.
They've danced through dirt, and mud, and rain,
Each scuff a laugh, each tear a gain.

They're wiser than the new ones bright,
With stories funny, love at fright.
In every crease, a memory stored,
They teach you life, without a chord.

So lace them tight, take the chance,
These worn-out shoes hold the best dance.
They'll lead you to joy, in an awkward stride,
With laughter echoing, friends by your side.

Hope from the Hearth

In the kitchen chair, naps are found,
Where crumbs and dreams are scattered around.
The hearth is warm, and so is the tea,
As grandma whispers some mystery.

She says the spatula can lead you far,
Cook up a treat, then eat like a star!
With flour on noses and giggles that spread,
Who knew from the kitchen, great tales are fed?

The dishes may pile and the soup may burn,
Yet hope rises up, each time we learn.
Even leftovers can bring such delight,
When served with laughter, it feels just right.

Fragments of Forgotten Dreams

In the attic lies a dusty box,
Full of failed plans and misfit socks.
A scrapbook page with a broken pen,
Dreams in fragments, but never again.

They whisper softly, 'What might have been?',
A croaky voice tells you to grin.
With silly doodles and a crumpled hat,
Who knew the past could make you laugh at that?

From failure's ashes, a giggle can bloom,
Turn 'what ifs' into a funny cartoon.
For every mishap deserves a cheer,
As each old scrap brings the future near!

Sunbeams Through Cracks

Tiny rays sneaking through the pane,
Like playful kittens, they tease and gain.
They dance on the floor, laughter in sight,
Filling the room with a quirky light.

In corners where shadows sketch a frown,
Sunbeams come bouncing, turning it around.
A tickle of warmth in the coldest of hearts,
Reminding us all, joy often starts.

So when life feels dim and thoughts start to roll,
Look for the cracks; that's where you'll stroll.
For even in gloom, there's a laugh to be found,
In beams of sunshine, let happiness abound.

Harmony in the Hopeless

In the sock drawer that's stacked so high,
Lies a lone sock with a patch of sky.
It dances with dreams of a laundry day,
Finding friends in the lint, come what may.

On the kitchen shelf with a mug half cracked,
A spoon sings the blues, feeling quite whacked.
With a teapot who whistles a comical tune,
They brew up laughter, morning to noon.

Under the bed where dust bunnies roam,
A lost Lego piece feels far from home.
It schemes with a pencil to craft a new game,
In the land of the chairs, they stoke the flame.

In the closet, there's coats who just want a chat,
Making jokes 'bout the cat who sat on the mat.
A patchwork of stories, stitched with delight,
Turns the mundane into sheer dynamite.

Lullabies of Lost Keys

Oh, the keys that jingle in the dark of night,
Whispering secrets with metallic delight.
They play hide and seek in the couch most deep,
Singing soft lullabies for those fast asleep.

A key to the lock of the fridge they find,
Dreaming of pickles, oh, how they're entwined!
Yet under a couch, they'd rather confide,
In stories of milk spills and a popcorn ride.

The pair of old keys clinks and clatters,
Arguing if life's about dreams or platters.
Together they giggle, making noise all night,
About the great exit from the wrong side of fright.

Each missing key is a tale in disguise,
With adventures in pockets and pizza surprise.
In a drawer or a purse, they hide and play,
Spreading joy as they're lost, come what may.

The Healing of Humble Things

A cereal box with a heart-shaped tear,
Starts a support group for breakfast fare.
They share tales of soggy, crunchy despair,
Finding laughter in crumbs, light as the air.

In the garden, a weed wears a crown of pride,
Proudly announcing it's here to abide.
Stirring up chaos with roots that entwine,
It grows outcast flowers, oh-so divine.

A pencil stub whispers, "I still can create,"
Encouraging paper to open the gate.
They sketch out a dream of a wild balloon,
Floating and laughing, dancing to tune.

A T-shirt with stains holds memories tight,
Stains of ice cream from a summer delight.
It chuckles at wear, proud of its fight,
For humble things shine with their own kind of light.

Fables from the Forest Floor

Amidst the leaves where shadows prance,
A little acorn dreams of chance.
With squirrels who waltz in a nutty ballet,
It chuckles at roots as they sway and play.

A twig on the ground finds steady friends,
With ants who gossip about life's trends.
Together they grill on a leaf for shade,
Tales of sunbathing, and lemonade made.

Under a log, where the mushrooms toast,
They celebrate life and make merry the most.
Each fan of laughter, each cap a delight,
Turns fungi's fate into a comical sight.

In the whispering woods, adventures ignite,
From acorns to ants, under soft starry light.
Finding joy in the trivial, giggles galore,
Life's little moments are worth asking for.

Lilies in the Mud

In a muddy patch, sunflowers dance,
A curious bug wearing underpants.
He wobbles around with a grin so wide,
In this messy world, he takes great pride.

Pig in the puddle, twirls with glee,
Takes a mud bath, as cheerful as can be.
A splashy party, oh what a sight,
Who knew the muck could feel so right?

Frogs croak tunes, oh what a band!
Each note a splash, across the land.
Mucking about with no cares in tow,
The lily's heart blooms where the wild things grow.

So next time you trip on a muddy lane,
Remember the joy and skip the pain.
In the thick of it all, you might just find,
A little joy, funny and unrefined.

Sagas of the Unseen

Under the fridge, a sock brigade,
They launch a coup, ready for a parade.
Stray crumbs cheer from the kitchen floor,
A riot of lint! Who could ask for more?

Behind the couch, lost dreams conspire,
Old remote controls plotting their hire.
Dust bunnies gather for a vast reunion,
Rendezvous of fluff, in joyful communion.

A rogue hairpin writes poetry of kin,
While paperclips fight some deep existential sin.
They rally and scribble on notes torn and old,
Tales of adventures just waiting to be told.

So when you lose sight of the grandeur ahead,
Look right within, where the mundane is spread.
You just might uncover an odyssey bright,
In the shadows of everyday, laughter takes flight.

Adventure in the Mundane

The toaster's on a quest for its long-lost bread,
Its crumb tray filled with stories, it said.
With each pop and jiggle, it shares old lore,
Of toasted powers and burnt-off scores.

A rogue mop swirls, performing a ballet,
Chasing dust bunnies in a playful way.
As spills rendezvous for a grand ol' feast,
This chaos creates a cleaning artist's beast.

The clock ticks loudly, spouting wise tales,
Each tock is a giggle, every tick never fails.
With the dawn of chores, heroes rise like bread,
In the daily grind, where fun often tread.

So grab your spatula, embrace your zest,
For even the simplest pursuits can be blessed.
In laughter we find, in every little chore,
The most epic adventures behind the pantry door.

Reflections in a Rusty Spoon

A rusty old spoon sits dulled and tired,
But when the sun shines, it beams with fire.
It reflects half-chewed culinary dreams,
And whispers of soups filling kitchen streams.

It dabbles in puddles of sauce and stew,
Turning drips into rivers, oh what a view!
A ladle of laughter, it scoops up the night,
Transforming some leftovers into pure delight.

The chef takes a bow, with spices galore,
But the spoon steals the show, forever wanting more.
"Oh, keep cooking!" it shouts, with quite the smug face,
As it watches the madness turn bland into grace.

So next time you hold a spoon worn and brown,
Remember the laughter, the upside-down crown.
In reflections so silly, you just might see,
The quirky joys found in mystery.

Inspiration in a Fleeting Glimpse

A cat on a fence, with a curious stare,
Catching the breeze like it just doesn't care.
It twirls and it jumps, with a flip and a flop,
Inspiration strikes when the mischief won't stop.

A squirrel in a hat, oh what a surprise,
Armed with some acorns and big, goofy eyes.
It dances on branches, a comical sight,
Who knew nature's jesters could ignite such delight?

A frog in a puddle, croaking a tune,
He's got all the rhythm, like a rockstar in June.
With each splash of water, he makes quite a scene,
Creativity blooms where it's mostly unseen.

The clouds overhead, they whisper and sway,
Mimicking dreams that have gone astray.
A giggle erupts from the wind as it blows,
In life's funny moments, true joy always grows.

Promises in the Potholes

A pothole so deep, a treasure to seek,
It swallows my shoe, oh what a critique!
Inside lies a promise, of mud and of grime,
I trip and I tumble, oh, isn't it prime?

A lost rubber duck, floats in the muck,
Its eyes wide with hope, oh what absolute luck!
In the chaos of asphalt, there's laughter to find,
Hidden jewels waiting to toy with your mind.

A worm wriggles past, in a slick little race,
Offering wisdom in its squishy embrace.
"Don't fret about sidewalks, just dance in the rain,
It's all about joy, not avoiding the pain."

So here's to the potholes, where blessings abound,
And laughter erupts from the dirt on the ground.
Life's silly mishaps, oh how they do gleam,
In the puddles of laughter, we find our sweet dream.

The Dance of Dust Motes

In a shaft of sunlight, they pirouette round,
Those tiny brown dancers, not making a sound.
Who knew that the dust could throw such a ball?
Swirling and twirling, they answer the call.

A sneeze interrupts, the ballet's on pause,
They scatter like confetti, just because!
But one little mote, with a wink in its flight,
Says, "This is the joy of a dust-dancing night!"

From window to window, they're lost in a trance,
In this hilarious dancing, life finds its chance.
So when you feel empty, just look up and see,
There's magic in dust, and it's wild and carefree.

Each sparkle a giggle, each swirl a delight,
In the mundane and small, there's wonder in sight.
So waltz with the dust, let your heart take a leap,
For laughter's the treasure that you'll find in heaps.

Grace Amongst the Gales

The wind howls loudly, ruffling my hair,
Yet flying my kite feels like dancing in air.
It flips with a flourish, a wild, funny sight,
Grace abounds here, amidst gale's playful bite.

A seagull zooms past, with a cheeky squawk,
Stealing my sandwich—as if it could talk!
With wings made for mischief, it flirts with my meal,
Life's little surprises, oh what a great deal!

As trees sway and bend, they show off their flair,
In a whirl of green leaves, they don't have a care.
They giggle and shake, in a raucous charade,
In grace, even gales can't break the parade.

So let's twirl with the wind, let our spirits take flight,
In the humor of chaos, we find pure delight.
For laughter and joy, like a kite in the sky,
Grace finds its home, as we soar—oh my!

Luminescence in the Litter

A crumpled chip bag, sparkling in the sun,
Who knew such glitter could come from a bun?
Ketchup packets glisten like jewels in the muck,
Treasure hunting here? Oh, I'm out of luck!

Finding lost coins amongst yesterday's fries,
Nuggets of glory beneath a fast-food guise.
Twirling around, making a dance with my find,
Bling in the trash? Well, isn't life kind?

A soda can glows like a gem in the grime,
Perhaps ancient artifacts caught in my rhyme?
I raise my glass to the junk on the street,
It's fashion week now, who knows who I might meet?

With laughter and shine, I stroll with my loot,
Who'd have thought litter could serve such a scoop?
In the chaos of waste, I find joy and glee,
Isn't it funny? Life's treasures are free!

Threads of Gold in Fabric

A sock with a hole could be thrown away,
But I see a cape for my cat, what do you say?
Button-eyed hero, she struts with delight,
Who knew a lost sock could bring such a sight?

Stitching and patching, I'm on a grand quest,
My pockets now bulging, I'm truly a mess.
Two blankets, a scarf, and a doll with no head,
I whip up a wonder from all that I dread.

Mixing and matching, with flair like a pro,
Turn trash into treasure — just watch my skills grow!
A pillow for dreams or a hat fit for kings,
In the fabric of life, creativity sings.

With laughter stitching tales and seams piled sky high,
Nothing's a waste when you dream and you try.
From snippets and ruins arise fields of gold,
Isn't it funny? The stories we hold!

Voices from the Vines

In the garden of weeds, where the wild things do thrive,
A cucumber whispers, "Come on, feel alive!"
The tomatoes are gossiping, what's ripening now?
The basil is dreaming of greener times somehow.

With zucchinis giggling, they dance in a line,
Swaying to secrets the sun loves to shine.
Radishes chatter about dirt's rich cuisine,
Sprouts offer wisdom, if you know what they mean.

From the tangled mess springs a comedy play,
While bugs with top hats entertain through the day.
Nature's own theater, no ancient oak bows,
Isn't it funny, their tales, we allow?

So dip in the dirt, hear the voices, don't fight,
A world full of laughter awaits if you bite.
In vines where the laughter and silliness churn,
Life's funny side shows just waiting to learn!

Adventure in the Abandoned

In an old, rusty truck, a mouse found his home,
He rolls out the red carpet, the world is his dome.
The spare tire swings like a tire-swing on high,
What a place for a party! Who needs the sky?

A cracked mirror reflects all the dreams of the past,
Echoes of laughter here, will it ever last?
Dust bunnies play tag, "You're it!" said a broom,
In the attic of "Who cares?" they dance in the gloom.

A chair with three legs thinks it's a ballet star,
While a creaky old floor leads the show from afar.
Picking up treasures where the lost things roam,
An adventure in junk, oh, it feels like home!

We dive in the crazy, where the silly holds sway,
With whispers of laughter, we brighten our day.
There's magic in ruins, if you are so bold,
Isn't it funny? What treasures unfold!

The Dancer in the Dust

In an old shoe, a rat found his groove,
Twisting and turning, he learned how to move.
With dust bunnies twirling, a party begun,
Who knew that a rodent could dance just for fun?

A mop in the corner joined in with a spin,
Their dance floor was messy but filled up with grin.
A broom tap-tapped softly, a rhythm so sweet,
In this quirky ballet, no one could beat!

The cat peeked inside, quite baffled in sight,
Three unlikely dancers, oh what a delight!
They laughed as they jived, not caring a bit,
In dust and in chaos, they found their perfect fit!

So here's to the moments that catch us off guard,
When life throws a curve, don't think it's too hard.
Embrace the absurd, let your spirit be bold,
In the tiniest corners, magic unfolds.

The Joy of Hidden Rails

A train set once lost under grandma's old bed,
Came back to life, and oh, what a spread!
The cat took the helm, the dog was the crew,
They chugged through the dust, like dreams coming true!

With no tracks to guide them, what fun they would seek,
Whiskers and woofs made for quite the unique.
They'd stop for a snack at a donut café,
Where treats spilled like laughter and brightened the day!

They zoomed past the curtains, through tangerine rooms,
Sailing through puddles of whimsical glooms.
Who knew such adventure lay just out of sight?
In the world of the hidden, everything's bright!

So when life feels tangled, no plan in your sight,
Remember that whimsy can set your heart right.
Find joy in the places that seem dull or plain,
Adventure is calling, jump on that train!

Stories from Silent Streets

In a quiet old town, where whispers don't shout,
The pigeons had secrets, no doubt about.
With monologues flapping, they narrated the day,
Of crumbs left as treasures, in their own feathered way.

A sidewalk cracked open held mysteries deep,
Where lost thoughts were stored, making passersby leap.
The cheese left by mice was a festival grand,
And seagulls were hired to play in a band!

The benches held gossip of souls yet untold,
While whispers of laughter around them would fold.
Each corner a canvas, each door the next stop,
In this silent hub, the stories won't stop!

So paint your own tales with whatever you find,
Through laughter and chatter, let your heart be unconfined.
The unnoticed is vibrant, the silent is bright,
In each quiet moment, we find our delight.

Spice in the Simple

In the kitchen were spices, all stacked like a dream,
A sprinkle of laughter, mixed into the cream.
A dash of confusion, a pinch of delight,
Cooking chaos became the family's night!

Grandpa grabbed garlic; he'd tossed it with flair,
While the kids danced around without any care.
The recipe called for an onion quite grand,
But instead, it was laughter they all had planned!

Cakes made of jelly and fries dressed in glee,
An upside-down salad, who knows what that could be?
But every bite tasted like pure, sunny smiles,
Simple life's treasure is found in the trials!

So when you feel busy and lost in the grind,
Remember the flavor of joy you can find.
With silliness garnished, the ordinary bright,
Life's spice comes alive when you feast with delight!

Hope Lurking in Abandoned Spaces

In a junkyard where old cars sleep,
A cat wearing shades starts to creep.
He pounces on tires, sings to the moon,
His disco ball dreams make even trash swoon.

A broken swing in a dusty yard,
Squeaks out tunes that aren't too hard.
With each creak, it tells tales of glee,
Of children who laughed, wild and free.

Underneath a rusted shed lies,
A garden of weeds, reaching for skies.
Yet hidden within, a flower peeks out,
Waving hello, banishing doubt.

In these corners where hope can roam,
A smile was found, making it home.
So if you're stuck in a mundane spot,
Look a bit closer; you'll find a lot.

The Beauty of a Rusty Key

A rusty key with a funny grin,
Claims it's the best in the lock-picking bin.
It dreams of doors that are long since sealed,
And giggles at secrets it feels revealed.

In a box of screws, it twirls with pride,
"Let me unlock that '90s ride!"
While others just chuckle, it takes the lead,
Unraveling the past like a mystery seed.

Hanging next to a moldy cheese bake,
It whispers, "I'm here for the fun to partake!"
The cheese just chuckles, "Oh key, you're a hoot,
But how do you plan to escape from this loot?"

So here's to the key, humble and old,
Chasing laughter instead of gold.
In places forlorn, it finds its own song,
For joy leaves footprints where it belongs.

Light After the Gloomy Hail

When clouds hang low and hail starts to drum,
A snail with a hat begins to hum.
It grooves on the grass like a pro on the stage,
While puddles around look like nature's rage.

The sun peeks out, a mischievous grin,
And raindrops dance like they're ready to spin.
With colors of laughter splashed all around,
Gloomy days itch to bounce to the sound.

A worm with a bowtie in a puddle bright,
Sways to the rhythm, morning to night.
"Don't worry!" it shouts, "We'll have fun on this trail!
We'll twirl through the mud, we'll dance after hail!"

So when skies seem dreary, and storms take their toll,
Remember the fun that can brighten your soul.
In every downpour, a party can spark,
Just look for the light; it's there in the dark.

Petals on the Windowsill

In a tiny pot with soil so thin,
A daisy peeks out with a cheeky grin.
"Look at me shine!" it proudly dreams,
While dust bunnies roll their eyes at its beams.

By the window, it catches the breeze,
Twirling to tunes that make it all tease.
"Don't judge my size! I'm a star of the show,
In this meager patch, I'm a flower pro!"

The sun whispers jokes to a sleepy old shoe,
As petals burst forth, making taffy-like goo.
"Dance while you can, don't let time slip away,"
Sings the sun to the petals, brightening the day.

So here on the sill, where dreams intertwine,
Beauty can flourish, both quirky and fine.
In the mundane moments, let laughter be known,
For joy is a bloom that you've always grown.

The Strength of the Scattered

A sock flies high, in the laundry worn,
It lands on the cat, who thinks she's adorned.
The broom's in the closet, on strike it's unseen,
Yet gathers the dust that swirls and dances, keen.

In the corner, a sandwich has taken a stand,
Declaring itself as the king of the bland.
The spoon hides a secret, unmoving and shy,
It dreams of a dinner, where it could be spry.

The table's quite wobbly, but what does it care?
It rocks with the rhythm of life, unaware.
With each bit of chaos, they find their own groove,
In the mess of the moment, they plan to improve.

So gather your treasures, though scattered they seem,
Each odd little item has a glorious dream.
In laughter and whimsy, the strength is revealed,
In the silliest corners, great power is healed.

The Poetry of the Unfit

The cactus wrote haikus, pricking with flair,
While daisies just giggled, tossed without care.
A snail in a race, oh what a grand jest,
With his slow little moves, he's truly the best.

The goldfish, a scholar, holds wisdom so deep,
But forgets what he's learned when he tries to sleep.
The lizard who sings in a most off-key tone,
Turns whispers of leaves into magic, well known.

The rock with a smile claims it studies the stars,
While ants tap dance around, avoiding the cars.
Each twist and each tumble brings stories anew,
In the oddest of places, creativity blew.

So admire the clumsy, the awkward, the meek,
For in every misfit, there's beauty unique.
With laughter in lines and a twist at the end,
The odd ones remind us to play and transcend.

The Ballet of the Barren

On a stage made of sand, the tumbleweeds twirl,
While rocks keep the rhythm, in a dust-coated whirl.
The sunburned cactus dons a tutu so bright,
As coyotes do pirouettes into the night.

The crickets provide the most chirpy of tunes,
While lizards take center, beneath the fat moons.
A pebble leaps high, then lands with a thud,
Creating a splash in the nearby dry mud.

The wind takes a bow, a true artist at heart,
Whispers of laughter, each gust is a part.
While tumbleweeds sway in a grand, carefree spin,
This barren ballet lets the wildness begin.

So cheer all those dancers with grit, grit, and grace,
For beauty can spring from the strangest of space.
In the dust and the drought, there's a show that's profound,
In the depths of the wasteland, great joy can be found.

Dreams in the Drought

In dusty old corners, a pipe dreams aloud,
Saying, 'Watch out, world, I'll form quite the crowd!'
A paperclip prances, in need of a mate,
Declaring sweet love for a scissor so straight.

The tumbleweed whispers its plans for the dance,
While sticks in the ground take a chance on romance.
A cactus serenades the bare, thirsty earth,
Hoping to spark a much-needed rebirth.

With raindrops as whispers that promise the night,
The stones start to giggle, oh what a delight!
A trash bag pirouettes on the hot summer breeze,
Finding the humor in life's little tease.

So search in the soil for the dreams that might sprout,
In the strangest of places, life raises a shout.
Amidst all the dryness, let laughter abound,
In the heart of the drought, great dreams will be found.

The Beauty of a Broken Mirror

In a shattered shard, I see my fate,
Reflections blurred, oh isn't it great!
Each little crack tells a tale so fun,
A face so silly, oh where'd I run?

My cat thinks it's a portal, oh what a joke,
Chasing her tail, she spins like smoke.
I giggle and laugh at this curious sight,
It's chaos, it's madness, but oh what delight!

My morning coffee spills, oh how it splashes,
In this bizarre world, reality clashes.
Each drip a reminder that life's quite absurd,
Through broken visions, joy's often stirred.

With shards of the past beneath my feet,
I dance like a fool, oh life can't be beat!
Embrace every fracture, every silly strife,
For laughter's the mirror that brightens this life.

Truths in the Tangle

In a mess of wires, my headphones twist,
A puzzle so complex, impossible to resist.
Each knot a reminder, laughter in tow,
As I wrestle with this, my patience on show.

Who knew that twinkles could cause such a fuss?
The lights in my house, a mix-up of trust.
With a flick of a switch, I summon a glow,
Oh dear, now it's disco, let's put on a show!

The spaghetti's a twister, oh such a sight,
Twirl it around, a marionette's flight.
With each little bite, flavors dance on my tongue,
In tangle and chaos, my heart ever young.

So here's to the mess, let's cheer and embrace,
For truth lives in tangles, in our human race.
With laughter and joy, we wander this path,
Finding gold in the chaos, we share in the laugh.

Fanfare from the Forgotten

In the attic there's dust, and a trumpet that wheezes,
Once played at parades, now collecting leaves and sneezes.
I blow a note, oh how it sputters,
The echoes of glory mixed with old butter!

Old toys in a box, a jester's delight,
A rubber chicken squeaks, it dances with might.
Each forgotten treasure, a relic of cheer,
Whispers of laughter, oh so sincere.

The old gramophone croaks, but gives it a go,
Spinning tales of music from long ago.
Each scratchy tune, like a secret unspun,
In the fanfare of dust, there's still so much fun!

So let's throw a bash for all that was lost,
Gather the laughter, forget about the cost.
In the cracks of the old, there's joy to be found,
In the forgotten corners, we laugh all around.

Hope Beneath the Hearth

Underneath the fire, the embers do dance,
With a marshmallow roast, the mice join the prance.
They nibble the crumbs, as I'm trying to snack,
A hilarious battle to take my treat back!

The soot on the wall tells a story so grand,
Of spaghetti nights gone wrong, and pies that were planned.
Flip a pancake too high, it thuds to the ground,
Oh, the laughter erupts, in chaos it's found.

With socks mismatched, I shuffle around,
Trying to find where my missing shoe's found.
The hearth's a warm chaos, a riotous glee,
In the heart of the home, it's wild and it's free!

So gather your friends, for the warmth of the night,
Underneath the hearth is a silly delight.
In the laughter and love, let the stories unfold,
In the quirks of our lives, our treasures are gold.

Secrets of the Sidewalk

Beneath my feet, a world so vast,
Cracks and grooves, a treasure cast.
A chewed up gum with a secret tale,
Of love and laughter without fail.

A lost sock waves from the curb,
Maybe it dreams of a life less suburban.
A candy wrapper's colorful flight,
Sparks joy in the sleepy night.

A button shines in the morning light,
Reminds me of a dance that felt so right.
The sidewalk's stories, oh, what a laugh,
In the mundane, we find the craft.

So take a stroll, look down with glee,
There's magic in the cracks, you'll see!
Embrace the oddities with a grin,
And let this quirky journey begin.

Unseen Journeys

A caterpillar on a mission to fly,
Hitching a ride, waving bye-bye.
On a leaf it dreams of its fate,
While ants parade, it's feeling great.

A mailbox whispers soft secrets inside,
Is it love letters, or junk to confide?
The postman grins at the notes he sends,
In the unseen, happiness blends.

A turtle slow on the sidewalk crawls,
With a tiny top hat, he's the king of it all.
He takes his time, no rush in sight,
In each slow step, there's pure delight.

Join the adventure, take the unplanned lane,
Where oddities thrive and laughter reigns.
Every step's a surprise, full of cheer,
In unseen journeys, joy is near.

Serendipity in Shadows

In a darkened corner, a raccoon does dance,
With a donut on his head, he spins at a glance.
His shadow winks, a mischievous sight,
As he prances about under the pale moonlight.

A stray cat joins in, tail high with flair,
Together they plot, whiskered little pair.
With a pounce and a leap, they claim the night,
Chasing dreams that are silly and bright.

Forgotten shoes whisper tales of woe,
Of marathons missed and places to go.
But they find joy in the dust, so sweet,
For shadows reveal what's simply a treat.

So dance with the shadows, have a laugh or two,
In the oddest places, bright sparks break through.
Serendipity lies in every odd view,
Just look close enough, and it reaches for you.

Treasures from Tattered Pages

An old book's spine creaks with history's sigh,
As pages flutter like birds in the sky.
Within it lies a recipe for pie,
And an accidental love note that makes you cry.

Forgotten poetry, a cat's haiku,
About chasing sunbeams and weather so blue.
A wilted flower pressed next to the door,
Reminds us that love can mean so much more.

Each tattered corner holds a riddle undone,
With doodles of spaceships and puns that are fun.
A scribbled doodle, a dream to unfurl,
In the margins, a whimsical world.

So dive into books, let laughter unfold,
In the tattered and torn, adventures are bold.
Every treasure you find brings smiles and glee,
In the pages of life, wild and free.

The Hidden Dance of Weeds in Concrete

In cracks where the sun barely peeks,
Little weeds have their awkward weeks.
They wiggle and shimmy, oh what a sight,
Dancing to rhythms of day and night.

No garden around, just grit and grime,
Yet these green rebels have perfect timing.
Their wild twirls make no gardener gloat,
But they're the best at the concrete tote!

With roots so stubborn, they won't be tamed,
A social media post should be framed!
"Look at us! We grow despite the odds!"
Champions of chaos, the campy little gods!

So, cheers to the weeds that thrive and persist,
In the harshest of places, they've got a twist.
Who needs a flower to brighten the scene?
When the bold little weeds put on a routine!

Echoes of Love in Forgotten Places

In an old parking lot, love letters lay,
Crushed by car tires, but they still say,
"I loved you in summer, 'neath stars so bright,"
Even rusting away, they still find light.

A bench by the dumpster has stories to tell,
Of lovers who shared more than just a spell.
They left bubblegum wrappers and little notes,
Under layers of filth where romance floats.

In shadows of buildings where nobody goes,
Whispers of passion still hang like clothes.
A napkin of dreams stuck deep in the grime,
Echoing giggles that froze in time.

So out of the trash, love finds a thread,
In odd little corners where few dare to tread.
Forget the posh places, they're overrated,
Just look in the lost, where affection's created!

Rebirth in the Ashes of Yesterday

From the ashes of burnt out dreams, we rise,
A charred barbecue pit holds our surprise.
In leftover embers, a sprout makes its stand,
As if it had plans that were utterly grand.

Once there was char, now there's a green,
Like a phoenix at a backyard cuisine.
We thought it was over, gone with the grill,
But nature just chuckles, "I'm here for the thrill!"

A wilted hot dog now blooms into joy,
In a space once filled with a sad little ploy.
Sizzling past remnants, a new tale is spun,
Of life from the ashes, and isn't it fun?

So let's raise a glass to all that is new,
Even when yesterday's vibes feel askew.
In the fried and the flamed, life still finds a way,
With a wink and a grin, let's seize the day!

Fragments of Light in a Lean-To

In the old lean-to, light spills like gold,
Between cracked boards, hidden gems unfold.
Dust motes are dancing in beams of the sun,
A party for shadows, oh what fun!

Forgotten corners may seem rather bleak,
But secrets of joy are what they seek.
Old chairs sit by, in the sun they will bask,
Whispers of laughter, the fun of a task.

A half-empty beer can is keeping it real,
Once a wild party, now a cozy meal.
Yet under the grime lies a spark of delight,
Just take a small peek, or maybe don't bite.

So raise up a toast to the lean-to of cheer,
With fragments of light that break up the drear.
In the oddest of spots, let joy find its place,
In the humble lean-to, find your happy space!

The Wisdom of a Withered Leaf

A leaf that has turned brown, oh so wise,
It tells tales of life with sighs and cries.
In the corners of the path, it lays still,
Reminding us, even gnarled, we can fulfill.

It flutters in the wind with a crooked grin,
Teaching us that fun can come from within.
So don't be too serious, life loves a jest,
Even when you're ragged, you're still at your best.

A leaf in the gutter, a sight quite absurd,
But wisdom's most often heard from the blurred.
It whispers of laughter, in every decay,
In nature's odd corners, joy finds a way.

So next time you see one, don't just scoff,
Befriend that old leaf, take your hat off.
For in the strangest places, truth takes its flight,
And teaches us all to embrace the delight!

Mismatched Socks and Hidden Truths

Two socks in the drawer don't even agree,
One's polka-dotted while the other's a spree.
But when they get together, oh what a sight,
Their dancing antics give a laugh every night.

They roam the floor boldly, with nary a care,
Defying all style, they form quite the pair.
Whispers of secrets they quietly share,
In each silly twist, a truth that's laid bare.

In the laundry's embrace, fun flourishes bright,
With each tumble they giggle, a silly delight.
So when life feels shuffled, and colors don't match,
Just think of those socks and the fun they dispatch.

Celebrate quirky, join in their charm,
For hidden in chaos is warmth, it's no harm.
Embrace every mismatch, with laughter and glee,
For life's little truths come in wild jubilee!

Songs from the Old Train Station

In the old train station, where echoes reside,
A banjo is strumming while lives coincide.
Passengers hurry, but the songs float afloat,
Mixing with laughter, a whimsical note.

A pigeon joins in with a cheeky coo,
While a man with a suitcase hums right on cue.
The clock ticks in time, but they don't seem to care,
As music dances lightly through the stale air.

Beneath creaky rafters, tales come alive,
Of journeys and laughter, they thrive and they strive.
It's here in the waiting, the mundane turned grand,
Unexpected moments weaving hand in hand.

So next time you're stuck at the station in gloom,
Just listen for laughter, let music consume.
For in every bustling, there's magic to find,
In the strums of old banjos, we're all intertwined!

Epiphanies Beneath the Quiet Bridge

Beneath a bridge quiet, where the waters glide,
Lies a pair of old shoes, where lost dreams abide.
Small fish swim below, in a playful ballet,
While a grumpy old frog croaks his wisdom each day.

With every ripple made, a giggle is grown,
From the secrets shared by the stones overthrown.
Life's grand revelations often stay under wraps,
Beneath humble bridges, away from mishaps.

So, gather around for the tales they recite,
Of love and of loss, of shadows and light.
In the whispers of water, the frogs croak their truth,
Finding laughter in places we once deemed uncouth.

Next time you're wandering, don't hurry on by,
Look for the jesters beneath the soft sky.
For even in silence, there are giggles to steal,
In the most unremarkable spots, we learn how to feel!

Nostalgia in a Nail

Once a shiny red nail, oh so bright,
Now it's bent and rusted, lost its fight.
But in its twisted way, it holds a tale,
Of swinging hammers and a childhood trail.

Underneath the porch, it sadly stays,
Reminds me of summer, long sunny days.
While the dog chased shadows and the cat feigned grace,
That nail's just a relic of a joyful place.

Clinging to memories, oh what a feat,
Turning dust and cobwebs to something sweet.
For laughter lives on in each dent and chip,
In the quirkiest places, it finds its grip.

So here's to the nail, a friend in disguise,
With its rusty old skin and its faded wise eyes.
In the quietest corners where we seldom tread,
Is where the funniest stories are often bred.

The Radiance of Rust

In the corner of the yard, a bike once grand,
Covered in rust, its glory has spanned.
With wheels full of dreams, now tangled in weeds,
It sparkles with history, in life it still leads.

Kids once rode high, with the wind in their hair,
Now it's a throne for a cat without care.
But when sunlight glints on the rusty old chain,
There's beauty in chaos, a laughter, a gain.

With squeaks and squawks, the memories fight,
Of races long gone on a warm summer night.
So here's to the rust, the old and the bold,
It radiates stories that never get old.

No shiny new handlebars or tires in place,
But a laughter-filled past to forever embrace.
In the awkwardness of life, in funny old crust,
We find joy in the old, in the rapture of rust.

Serenity by the Sewage

Down by the brook where the sewers flow,
A peaceful abode, or maybe not so.
With a whiff of adventure, and a splash of grime,
Serenity's found, oh what a crime!

The frogs hold court on their slippery throne,
While the fish gossip in tones quite unknown.
But amidst the odd smells, a calm seems to dwell,
A humorous charm, who could ever tell?

A picnic of pigeons with crumbs flying high,
Even the raccoons look sharp as they sly.
There's laughter in nature, if you stick around,
In this quirky oasis, joy can be found.

Though the waters may murmur in somewhat foul tunes,
There's a symphony blooming under crescent moons.
Life's funny in corners where we seldom stretch,
Serenity's found where we least expect.

Finding Gold in Grime

In a puddle of muck, shines a glint so bright,
Is it treasure or trash? Oh, what a sight!
With a squint and a smile, I lean down to see,
A coin from the past, just laughing at me.

In the dirt of the road where the sidewalk ends,
Lies a trinket of childhood, where mischief ascends.
With sticky old gum and a handful of grit,
Gold's not just diamonds; it's every fun bit.

A crumpled-up map with a heart drawn in ink,
Hints at the days when we'd gather and think.
With giggles and whispers, adventures unfurled,
Grime's just a canvas for a glorious world.

So here's to the scraps, the dirt, and the mess,
In the laughter of treasure, we find our success.
From filth to fond memories, let spirits climb high,
For in mud and in muck, the greatest joys lie.

www.ingramcontent.com/pod-product-compliance
Lightning Source LLC
Chambersburg PA
CBHW051645160426
43209CB00004B/791